KU-638-306

CONNECTING CULTURES THROUGH FAMILY AND FOOD

The Thai Family Table

By H.W. Poole

MASON CREST

Mason Crest
450 Parkway Drive, Suite D
Broomall, PA 19008
www.masoncrest.com

© 2019 by Mason Crest, an imprint of National Highlights, Inc.

All rights reserved. No part of this publication may be reproduced or transmitted in any form or by any means, electronic or mechanical, including photocopying, recording, taping, or any information storage and retrieval system, without permission in writing from the publisher.

Printed and bound in the United States of America.

First printing
9 8 7 6 5 4 3 2 1

Series ISBN: 978-1-4222-4041-0
Hardback ISBN: 978-1-4222-4052-6
EBook ISBN: 978-1-4222-7750-8

Produced by Shoreline Publishing Group LLC
Santa Barbara, California
Editorial Director: James Buckley Jr.
Designer: Tom Carling
Production: Patty Kelley
www.shorelinepublishing.com
Front cover: Davidf/iStock.com

Library of Congress Cataloging-in-Publication Data
Names: Poole, Hilary W., author. Title: The Thai family table / by H.W. Poole.
Description: Broomall, PA : Mason Crest, [2018] | Series: Connecting cultures through family and food | Includes bibliographical references and index.
Identifiers: LCCN 2017053438| ISBN 9781422240526 (hardback) | ISBN 9781422277508 (ebook) Subjects: LCSH: Cooking, Thai--Juvenile literature. | Thai Americans--Food--Juvenile literature. | Thai Americans--Social life and customs--Juvenile literature. | Thailand--Social life and customs--Juvenile literature.
Classification: LCC TX724.5.T5 P67 2018 | DDC 641.59593--dc23 LC record available at https://lccn.loc. gov/2017053438

QR Codes disclaimer:

You may gain access to certain third party content ("Third-Party Sites") by scanning and using the QR Codes that appear in this publication (the "QR Codes"). We do not operate or control in any respect any information, products, or services on such Third-Party Sites linked to by us via the QR Codes included in this publication, and we assume no responsibility for any materials you may access using the QR Codes. Your use of the QR Codes may be subject to terms, limitations, or restrictions set forth in the applicable terms of use or otherwise established by the owners of the Third-Party Sites. Our linking to such Third-Party Sites via the QR Codes does not imply an endorsement or sponsorship of such Third-Party Sites, or the information, products, or services offered on or through the Third- Party Sites, nor does it imply an endorsement or sponsorship of this publication by the owners of such Third-Party Sites.

Contents

Introduction 6

1. Getting Here 10
SNACKS AND STREET FOOD........................22

2. Settling In.................................... 24
SOUPS AND SALADS................................ 34

3. Connecting 36
THE MAIN COURSE............................. 48

4. Reaching Back 50
DESSERT 58

Find Out More 62

Series Glossary of Key Terms...................63

Index/Author.................................... 64

KEY ICONS TO LOOK FOR

 Words to Understand: These words with their easy-to-understand definitions will increase the reader's understanding of the text, while building vocabulary skills.

 Sidebars: This boxed material within the main text allows readers to build knowledge, gain insights, explore possibilities, and broaden their perspectives by weaving together additional information to provide realistic and holistic perspectives.

 Educational Videos: Readers can view videos by scanning our QR codes, providing them with additional educational content to supplement the text. Examples include news coverage, moments in history, speeches, iconic moments, and much more!

 Text-Dependent Questions: These questions send the reader back to the text for more careful attention to the evidence presented here.

 Research Projects: Readers are pointed toward areas of further inquiry connected to each chapter. Suggestions are provided for projects that encourage deeper research and analysis.

 Series Glossary of Key Terms: This back-of-the-book glossary contains terminology used throughout this series. Words found here increase the reader's ability to read and comprehend higher-level books and articles in this field.

Introduction

Thailand is a nation in Southeast Asia, flanked by Myanmar on the west and by Laos and Cambodia on the east; it also shares a border with Malaysia to the south. The word *thai* means "free," and Thai people will tell you with pride that theirs is the only South Asian country that was never colonized by a Western power. The country was called Siam by outsiders, until the name was officially changed in 1948. But some remnants of the old name still exist: For example, Siamese cats were bred from cats that were native to Thailand.

Officially, Thailand is divided into 76 provinces, each with its own governor and administration. However, it's often said (only somewhat jokingly) that there is one additional province: Los Angeles, California. Los Angeles and its surrounding communities are home to the largest community of Thai people anywhere outside of Asia. Roughly two-thirds of all Thai Americans call Southern California home.

The existence of Thai communities anywhere outside Thailand is fairly new. Unlike countries with long histories of emigration—Ireland, for example, or Greece—Thai people have only been moving to other countries in large numbers since the mid-1960s. People of Thai ancestry are still sorting out precisely what it means to be a Thai American, Thai Canadian, or Thai Australian, simply because the entire phenomenon is only about 50 years old.

We do know that many of the first Thai people to arrive in the United States worked hard to become as American as possible, as quickly as possible. Many were married to US military personnel, which means they joined American families as soon as they stepped off the plane. Others were doctors and nurses, who were highly educated and eager to become medical professionals in the United States. The desire to fit in was often quite strong.

On the other hand, some Thai

immigrants came to the United States in search of economic or educational opportunities and viewed the United States as a place to work—to them, America was never intended to be home the way Thailand had been.

Interestingly, whether these pioneer immigrants were eager to assimilate (which means to integrate into a larger culture) *or* rejected the idea completely, they all tended to view life in America as an

Thai restaurants are not hard to find in American and European cities.

either/or situation. You either abandoned your old self and became as American as you could, or you held tightly to your Thai roots and remained essentially a long-term visitor to the United States.

In either case, keeping a connection to one part of your Thai roots—food and dining—was important. The spread of Thai food in the United States is directly tied to the growing number of Thai people emigrating in recent decades.

In recent years, a third path has emerged, particularly among younger people. They were born in the United States but feel curious about the land their parents left behind. Rather than rejecting either culture, they are trying to forge a path that combines the best of both worlds: a new, Thai American identity.

Getting Here

Kao Kalia Yang was just six years old when she immigrated to America with her family. She and her older sister were both born in Ban Vinai Refugee Camp in Thailand. Everything about their new lives seemed strange at first—from the smells to the food, from the tall streetlights along roads to the "click, click" sound of women's high heels on hard floors. Even sleeping in a multistory building was foreign to young Kao, but it was also exciting. "The idea of sleeping on air . . ." she wrote later, "felt like something magical."

Adjusting to a new country would not be easy for the Yang family. But even so, Kao was eager to embrace whatever lay ahead. "America was before me," she recalled. "My mother and father were close by me, and the world was open."

Words to Understand

emigration   to leave one's birth country and live somewhere else (compare to immigration, which means to go to a country)

exclusion   to keep someone out or deny them access

presentation   here, the style in which food is plated and served

This family was one of many from Thailand who moved from refugee camps to a welcome reception in Minnesota.

A Brief Introduction to Thai Cuisine

Thailand is a fairly small country—a bit smaller than the state of Texas—with a population of about 68 million. But the nation has had an outsized influence on the world of food, and Thai cuisine is one of the most popular types anywhere.

The unique flavors and aromas of Thai cuisine blend many different influences. A thousand years of cultural exchange between Thailand and India, its northwestern neighbor, resulted in curries becoming one of the most important categories of Thai dishes. Another vital cooking technique, stir-frying, was introduced to Thailand hundreds of years

Stir-frying is a part of much of Thai cuisine, whether on the street as shown here, or in restaurants and private kitchens.

ago by the Chinese. And that vital Thai ingredient, the chili pepper, was brought to Thailand by Portuguese merchants.

In his book *Thai Food*, author and chef David Thompson compares the histories of the tomato and the chili pepper as a way of explaining Thailand's attitude toward outside influences. When explorers brought tomato plants from the New World back to Europe, the plants were widely

The Five Flavors

Specific ingredients are used to create the all-important five flavors of Thai cuisine. Here are just a few:

- Sweet: different types of sugar, including palm and coconut sugars
- Sour: lemongrass, kaffir lime leaves (below)
- Spicy: chili peppers
- Salty: fish sauce, soy sauce
- Bitter: bitter melon, leaves of the cassod tree

believed to be poisonous. It took about 200 years for tomatoes to be accepted by European cooks. By contrast, when the chili was introduced to Thailand by Portuguese traders, it was adapted within just one generation, and the chili quickly became an essential component of Thai cooking.

Thai food gets its heat from chilis, but it's important to understand Thai food is more than just spicy. The philosophy of Thai cuisine is built on the notion of balancing five essential flavors: sweet, sour, salty, bitter, and spicy (see box on page 13). Thai American food tends to avoid the more bitter or sour flavors, because many Americans don't enjoy those. But ideally, Thai dishes should balance these flavors equally.

Beautiful **presentation** is another important aspect of Thai cuisine. For example, fruits and vegetables are sometimes carved into delicate flowers or other pleasing shapes. The emphasis on presentation is partly due to the fact that, historically, styles and trends in cooking used to begin

Thai food basics

in the kitchens of Thailand's royal family. Chefs hoped to please the king with ever more elaborate meal presentations. The fashionable styles would gradually spread to the rest of the population.

The Thai and the *Farang*

Thailand was never colonized by European powers, but that's not to say it was unfriendly to the *farang* (the Thai word for white-skinned Europeans). The first foreigners to visit Thailand—then called the Kingdom of Ayutthaya—were probably Portuguese diplomats who arrived in 1511, and the Thai have been trading with Europeans ever since. And they were not only willing to do business with *farang*; they were open-minded about

This painting of an ancient Thai temple hangs in a museum in Bangkok.

European culture in general. (Even if they didn't necessarily approve of it! See box below for more.)

Throughout the 1700s and 1800s, Thailand was careful to maintain good relations with both Great Britain and France while those countries fought for control of Southeast Asia. The French were colonizing Laos and Vietnam while the British were in control of Myanmar (then known as Burma). Thailand became a buffer zone between the two superpowers. And unlike China, which saw significant amounts of **emigration** in the mid-1800s, there was minimal emigration out of Thailand until the second half of the 1900s.

The Guests Are Not Impressed

In 1686, King Narai of Siam sent people to France to meet with King Louis XIV. The group was led by Siam's top ambassador, Kosa Pan (right), and his goal was to establish an alliance between the two countries. The French court fell in love with the Siamese visitors, but it seems the affection wasn't entirely returned—at least not when it came to French food.

In his diary, Kosa Pan complained that French cuisine is comprised of "few spices and much meat," and that, in his opinion, the French opted for quantity of food over quality of ingredients. He also noted that the French drank quite a lot of wine, a habit that Kosa Pan assumed was an attempt to mask the tastelessness of their meals.

Leaving Thailand

Only a very small number of people from Thailand came to the United States before World War II, but two who did made a big impression (see page 18). A few individuals aside, the first noteworthy emigration didn't take place until the 1950s. That's when Thai visitors were welcomed in Australia under a development program called the Colombo Plan. Named for the site of its 1950 signing in Colombo, Sri Lanka, the plan was designed to encourage economic and cultural exchanges among Asia-Pacific countries. One result was an increase in the number of Asian students who traveled to study at Australian universities. In most instances, the students were

Thanks to the Colombo Plan, Thai immigration to Australia (home of Sydney's famous opera house, above) increased, starting in the 1960s.

expected to go home after their studies were completed, but there were exceptions. Asian students who married Australians, for instance, were allowed to stay. As a result, the Colombo Plan marks the beginning of a small but gradually increasing Thai community in Australia.

Thai emigration to the United States, on the other hand, was kick-started not by diplomacy but by war. America was involved in what became the Vietnam War by the early 1960s. Thailand was aligned with the anti-Communist forces in that conflict, and let the United States establish numerous military bases around the country. By the late 1960s, Thailand

Chang and Eng

The very first Thai immigrants may have been Chang and Eng, conjoined twins who were born near Bangkok in 1811. The brothers were permanently connected to each other at the chest. They toured the world, displaying themselves as "curiosities," and becoming wealthy celebrities in the process. In fact, it's due to Chang and Eng's great fame that all conjoined twins used to be known as Siamese twins. (Their parents were ethnically Chinese and so, ironically, in their birth country Chang and Eng were known as Chinese twins, not Siamese.)

had become a wartime home to some 25,000 American military personnel.

The presence of so many Americans had a big impact on Thailand and its culture. In terms of food, the soldiers brought with them their fondness for hamburgers and Cokes. They also inspired the invention of American fried rice, which adds ketchup to the original dish. Some US soldiers married Thai women and brought their wives home after the war. This was the beginning of a Thai presence in the United States.

One of these soldiers was a Marine named Franklin Duckworth. He married Lamai Sompornpairn, a young woman who was working at her parents' store at the time. In 1968, they had a daughter, Ladda Tammy Duckworth, who would go on to serve in the Iraq War and to represent Illinois as the first Thai American senator.

Tammy Duckworth spent her childhood traveling around Southeast Asia with her parents, who worked for various government-run refugee

Thai people in Sydney, Australia

programs. Despite the tremendous destruction and loss of life that resulted from the Vietnam War, young Tammy was struck by the fact the United States was still viewed as a beacon of opportunity everywhere she went. "People wanted to be like us," she told an interviewer in 2016. "People wanted to do business with Americans and they wanted to send their kids to American schools."

Coming to America

For decades, people from Asian countries were forbidden to enter the United States due to a series of **exclusion** acts. The first of these laws was the Chinese Exclusion Act of 1882, but after that the laws were expanded to keep out people from more and more Asian countries. It wasn't

Thai Town signs in Los Angeles point visitors to a part of town where they will find Thai food and culture.

until the 1960s that these laws were changed, and the first group of Thai immigrants was admitted into the United States in 1966.

Many of these so-called pioneer immigrants went to Southern California, and over time that community has continued to grow. A second, colder location for many immigrants is the Minneapolis–St. Paul area. This is where Kao Kaila Yang and her family ended up in 1987. New York, Nevada, Illinois, and Texas also have sizable Thai communities. Until 1970, there were only about 5,000 Thai Americans. But the community has grown rapidly since then. The 2010 census found 237,583 people of Thai descent in the United States; that's a 58 percent increase from the previous census in 2000.

Text-Dependent Questions:

1. What are the five flavors of Thai cuisine?

2. Why were there so few Thai immigrants to the United States before the 1960s?

3. Who is Tammy Duckworth?

Research Project:

Find out more about the exclusion acts that were part of US law in the first half of the 20th century. What arguments were made for and against these acts? How are these arguments similar to or different from current immigration debates?

SNACKS AND STREET FOOD

Thai meals don't have an appetizer course the way European-style meals do. But snacks are a huge part of Thai cuisine. According to Chef David Thompson, these foods are referred to as *aharn wang*, or "outside the meal." In Thailand, outside-the-meal snacks are usually purchased from street vendors, rather than made at home.

Pad Thai

If you've only tried one type of Thai food, it's probably this peanuty stir-fried noodle dish. In the United States, pad thai is served with shrimp, bean sprouts, and a few pieces of fried tofu. In Thailand there's more variety in the way pad thai is prepared. But the dish is not really a traditional Thai food; it was created in 1938, shortly after the Thai monarchy was forced out of power. Pad thai carts were sent all over to introduce citizens to a new, patriotic way of eating. In Thailand, pad thai is popular as a street food, while in the United States, it's easily the most-ordered Thai dish in restaurants.

Spring Rolls

Although people in Thailand don't really eat appetizers, Thai restaurants in the United States serve lots of them. That's because restaurant owners understand that their customers expect to see them on the menu. But although spring rolls are common at Thai restaurants, these Asian-style appetizers are actually Chinese in origin.

Kao Pad (Fried Rice)

Originally Chinese, fried rice dishes have been popular in Thailand since at least the 1800s. Kao pad is cooked quickly in a wok with oil, egg, and a variety of other ingredients. Just about anything you like can be added to kao pad, from deep-fried fish to pork to crab to bitter melon. It's served with a spicy condiment called prik nam pla, *which is made from diced chilis, fish sauce, and lime juice.*

Kai Jeow (Thai Omelette)

Omelettes are very popular street food in Thailand and are eaten at any time of day. Unlike in the West, eggs are not thought of only as a breakfast food only. Thai omelettes tend to be crispy on the outside and soft on the inside, and they're usually eaten with some sort of chili paste or a hot sauce such as sriracha.

Maeng Da (Water Bugs)

A lot of Thai street foods are catching on in the West, but deep-fried water bugs may be a step too far for most. But maeng da *are actually a very important part of Thai cuisine. If you are brave enough, you eat* maeng da *by pulling off the wings, separating the body from the head, and sucking the meat out of the body. Yum!*

Settling In

When Kao Kalia Yang was packing to move to America, she had a lot of worries. One of her big concerns was what the food would be like. She felt certain that she wouldn't like American food at all. Her favorite meal in those days was a soup that her mother made with ground beef, tomatoes, lemongrass, and rice. Would she ever get to eat that again, she wondered. "I asked [my mother] if there was even rice in America and would we really be eating soup at all? Didn't Americans just eat chicken sandwiches?"

Her mother assured Kao that there would still be soup in America. She made a point of packing the soup pot, just to prove it.

Words to Understand

abundance   a very large amount of something

consistency   here, refers to how thick or thin a liquid is

ethnic cleansing   forcibly removing or killing members of an ethnic group

sociologist   someone who studies societies and how they function

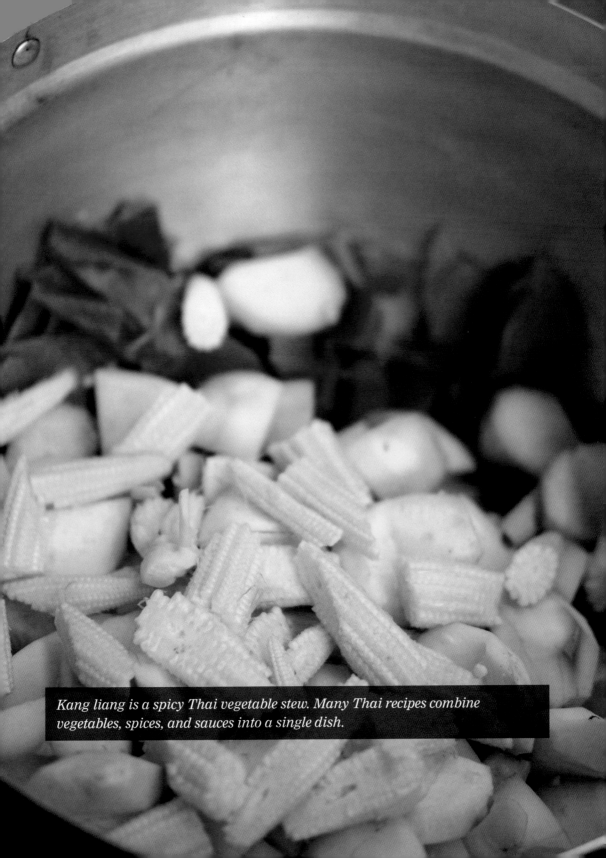

Kang liang is a spicy Thai vegetable stew. Many Thai recipes combine vegetables, spices, and sauces into a single dish.

Seeking Opportunities

No two immigration stories are exactly the same. Every person or family has their own reasons for leaving home and coming to the United States. But if we look at the past 50 years of Thai immigration to America, we can identify a few broad trends.

Educational opportunity has long been an important factor inspiring Thai people to leave home. As we've already mentioned, some of the very first Thai emigrants were students who went to Australia to study. That trend has continued with immigration to the United States as well. Thai people tend to value education a great deal, and since American universities are well respected around the world, it's not unusual for Thai students to want to attend.

Some young Thai people come to America to expand their college choices.

Thai parents who immigrate to the United States also tend to have big educational dreams for their kids. Jirayut Latthivongskorn was just nine years old when he emigrated from Thailand with his parents. They both took jobs at Thai restaurants, where they worked extremely long hours every day. Sometimes Jirayut would offer to help out, maybe get

Thai Restaurants

Many of the immigrants mentioned in this book have something in common besides being Thai—they got their first American jobs in Thai restaurants. Restaurant kitchens are often staffed with immigrants because the work is hard and the wages are low; you need a lot of determination to succeed there, but determination is something that recent immigrants tend to have in **abundance**.

Ironically, many Thai immigrants have to be taught how to prepare "Thai food" as restaurants serve it, which is not always the same as how the food was prepared at home. (See page 44 for more on the types of changes Thai American cooks have made to traditional recipes.) What's more, not every immigrant arrives with cooking experience. Today, for example, a woman named Thippawan "Tip" Shutts runs a successful food truck called Mobile Thai Kitchen in St. Robert, Missouri. But she didn't know how to cook when she arrived in the United States in 2014; she had to learn while working at a Thai restaurant. Why? Because back in Thailand, the village Shutts grew up in didn't have access to refrigeration.

a job of his own. But his parents always said no. "Don't worry and do *your* job," they would tell him. More than anything, Jirayut's parents wanted their son to get a good education, and that was the only "job" they wanted him to have.

In addition to educational opportunities, economic opportunities are another key driver of Thai immigration to America. In his memoir, *Talk Thai*, Ira Sukrungruang talks about growing up in Chicago in the 1980s. The adults he knew "viewed America only as a workplace," he writes. "America provided jobs. America provided opportunities Thailand couldn't."

Many Thai immigrants arrive in the United States eager to make their mark, but they often have to start at the bottom and work their way up. Satathana-An "Pin" Chanda left her home in Udon Thai Province, to look for work in the United States. She had a master's degree in engineering, but when she arrived, she had to take a job in a Thai restaurant in the Baltimore area. But her dream was always to put her degree to work in

Educational opportunities have attracted many young Thais to the West.

the United States. Similiarly, Ittikorn Hunsagul is a recent immigrant to Seattle; he was an architect in Chiang Mai, Thailand, but as of 2016 he was working as a dishwasher at a Thai restaurant while he studied English. "I need my son to grow up here," Ittkorn told *The Seattle Times*, "I hope he has a good future. . . . He can do whatever he wants to do. Anything."

Seeking Safety

Sociologists describe things like economic and educational opportunities as "pull" factors for immigration. In other words, people are drawn to the United States in search of particular things, such as better jobs. But there are also "push" factors for immigration, meaning things that drive people from their home countries. And unfortunately, a great many Thai immigrants have come to the United States due to the push factors of war and **ethnic cleansing**.

Inside a Thai restaurant

We have already introduced you to Kao Kalia Yang and her family, who immigrated from Thailand in 1987. The Yangs are members of an ethnic group called the Hmong (pronounced "Mong"), who ended up in Thai refugee camps after fleeing violence in Laos. The 2010 census reported that there were about 260,000 Hmong refugees living in the United States. Many Hmong, like Kao, were born in Thailand and even speak Thai, but they usually view themselves as Hmong rather than Thai.

There is yet another group of immigrants from Thailand who are members of another ethnic group, the Karen ("Kah-REN"). Like the Hmong, the Karen also were forced to flee their homes due to ethnic cleansing—but they were fleeing Myanmar (Burma). Also like the Hmong,

The Karen people were forced into refugee camps in Thailand like this one by the policies of neighboring Myanmar.

A Refugee Spices Things Up

When it comes to condiments, Americans tend to be pretty straightforward. We like salt and pepper on the table, a bottle of ketchup, and maybe BBQ sauce or salsa. But in the past decade, a new bottle has started appearing on more and more US tables: sriracha (si-RAH-cha). This hot sauce, which is both sweet and spicy, has its roots in Thailand.

Sriracha was invented in 1949 by a Thanom Chakkapak, who lived on Thailand's eastern coast. Initially, she simply made the sauce to use in her own cooking. But her guests always ended up asking for extra, so she started making it in larger and larger batches. Because she used local peppers to make the sauce, she named it after her hometown, Si Racha. It wasn't long before the sauce, which is sometimes also spelled *sriraja*, was being used all over Thailand.

The Thai version of sriracha has a somewhat thinner **consistency** than the one we eat in the United States. The flavor is a bit sweeter and not quite as hot. In Thailand, sriracha is often used on omelettes, in soup, and as a dipping sauce.

The story doesn't end there. In 1978, a ship called *Huy Fong* left Vietnam, carrying thousands of refugees who were fleeing the country after the war. One of those refugees, David Tran, ended up in Los Angeles. He began making his own version of sriracha to spice up his *pho* (a Vietnamese noodle soup). The hobby quickly turned into a successful business. Over the years, people have advised Tran to make the sauce less hot, add tomatoes, or tweak it other ways. But Tran has always refused to compromise. "Hot sauce must be hot," he says. "If you don't like it hot, use less. We don't make mayonnaise here." And it certainly seems like Tran was right. Huy Fong sells around 20 million bottles of sriracha every year.

many young Karen immigrants were born in Thailand's refugee camps. But again, even the Karen who were born within Thailand's borders view themselves as more Karen than Thai. More than 150,000 Karen refugees were admitted into the United States from 2006 to 2016; that's about a quarter of all refugees who arrived in America in that period.

Hmong and Karen refugees have also ended up in Australia. For example, the parents of Nouer Soe Pah Eh, who goes by the name Noble, fled to Thai refugee camps from Myanmar in the 1980s, and they were finally relocated to Canberra, Australia, in 2009. "They are terrorists," Noble said of the military. "The Burmese soldiers were fighting our people and killed our people. They were notorious for attacking my people and

Karen people who have settled in the United States have brought their culture with them and share it with their new neighbors.

taking everything in our house. My families were scared of them and moved to Thailand before I was born."

The quality of life in the refugee camps can vary a great deal; some people remember their experiences fondly, while others don't at all. Noble, for example, recalls the camp primarily as "boring," and says he was eager to get out and go to Australia. On the other hand, Aye Aye Win, a young Karen refugee who now lives in St. Paul, Minnesota, remembers enjoying the camp because she was allowed to play in the forest and at a nearby waterfall. She also recalls usually having enough food to eat. But many other refugees were not so lucky and often went hungry.

In 2012, one Karen refugee told Human Rights Watch: "It is so strict to live here [in the camp]. There is nothing to do. I am not allowed to go outside the camp. There is no job, no work. So much stress and depression. I feel that I am going to go crazy here."

Text-Dependent Questions:

1. What are push and pull factors for immigration?

2. Who are the Hmong?

3. Where do Karen refugees come from?

4. Who invented sriracha?

Research Project:

Visit a Thai restaurant near you and try some of the dishes mentioned in this book. Do the dishes achieve the desired balance of five flavors? Which ones are most appealing to you? Which seem the most foreign? Why do you think that is?

SOUPS AND SALADS

Although there's no soup or salad course, soups and salads do play a huge role in Thai cuisine—it's just that they are served along with everything else, rather than separately. You can expect to see lots of soups and salads on any Thai American restaurant menu.

Som Tum (Green Papaya Salad)
In this sour but delicious dish, ingredients such as garlic, peanuts, and chilis are pounded with a mortar and pestle, and then mixed with lime juice and fish sauce to make a dressing. This dressing, which can be mildly spicy or very spicy depending on the type of chilis used, is served over tomatoes, beans, and grated, unripened papaya. (If papayas aren't available, the dish is sometimes made with shredded cabbage instead.)

Tom Yum (Hot and Sour Soup)
This soup is known for its combination of spicy and sour flavors. To make it, you begin with a basic broth and then add some iconic Thai ingredients: kaffir lime leaves and lemongrass. Tom yum is most commonly served with prawns (shrimp), but beef, pork, or chicken is sometimes used instead.

Tom Kha Gai (Chicken and Coconut Soup)
Another classic Thai soup, tom kha gai *is made with coconut milk. It has some of the same ingredients as* tom yum *(like lemongrass and kaffir lime leaves), but it tends to be much less spicy. It can also be made with shrimp instead of chicken, or prepared vegetarian-style with ingredients such as tofu and mushrooms.*

Larb Gai (Chicken and Herb Salad)
Larb *(or larp) is a salad made from meat, herbs such as basil and mint, as well as other vegetables, such as onions. Traditionally, the meats in* larb *are not cooked; they are tossed together with a spicy dressing made from chilis and lime juice. Because consuming raw meat raises health concerns for many diners,* larb *in Thai restaurants is usually cooked. The chicken in* larb gai *may be stir-fried before it's put in the salad, or it might be put in the dressing raw and then the whole salad is simmered on the stove for a few minutes.*

Phla Goong (Cured Shrimp Salad)
In Thai, phla *(or pla), means "cured." Cured salads are very popular in Thai cuisine:* phla goong *is made with shrimp and is probably the best known. But there are many other types, such as* phla mu *with pork.*

Connecting

In *Talk Thai*, Ira Sukrungruang writes about a challenge that will be familiar to many immigrant kids: surviving the lunchroom. "Aunty Sue packed my Muppets lunch box with fried rice, a hard-boiled egg … and coconut-flavored pop. As soon as I unwrapped the foil, the smell of garlic and soy sauce wafted into the room; some of the kids complained my lunch smelled like poo."

Food is a hugely important signpost for culture and identity. Ira was born in the United States, which means he was every bit as American as the mean kids in the lunchroom. But the soy sauce in his lunch box immediately marked him as an outsider to the other kids.

Words to Understand

acclimate   to get used to something

accommodation   as used here, a compromise

collectivist a situation in which the group takes priority over the individual

intonation   the inflection or pitch of a person's speaking voice

For some Thai immigrants, school lunchtime can be a particular culture shock, as children find they can't always get meals they are used to.

Kao Kalia Yang recalls that after they moved to Minnesota, her mother attended night classes designed to help the family **acclimate** to American culture. One important skill her mother learned? How to make peanut butter and jelly sandwiches for her daughters.

Building Community

The first significant wave of Thai immigrants arrived in the United States in 1966. Many of these immigrants were educated and already spoke at least some English. Others were married to Americans—in particular, to US military personnel—which meant that even if their English was not great initially, they arrived with a support system already in place. But even so, the transition was not always easy!

One challenge was finding the ingredients to make the meals that reminded them of home. "Usually we shopped at Chinatown," Marasri

Going to a Thai market with Jet Tila

Tilakamonkul told a reporter later, "but they didn't have the ingredients the way Thais cook." So in 1972, the Tilakamonkul family did something about it and opened the Bangkok Market in East Hollywood. "My husband saw the opportunity," Tilakamonkul recalled, "so he decided that we should open the market right now." The market was the only place where Thai immigrants could buy ingredients like lemongrass and kaffir lime leaves, which are essential for Thai recipes but were nearly impossible to find in the United States at the time.

Bangkok Market quickly became much more than just a grocery store—it also became the center of Thai life in Los Angeles. For example, because there was no *wat* (Thai Buddhist temple) at the time, if someone

The Bangkok Market became not only a place to shop for Thai immigrants in Los Angeles, it became a kind of community center.

in the community died, there was nowhere to hold a funeral. Bangkok Market would shut down so the funeral could be held there.

In 1978, the Tilakamonkul family opened the first Thai restaurant in California. "I was born into the 'first family' of Thai food in Los Angeles," their eldest son said later. That kid, who packed groceries at Bangkok Market and did his homework at a table in the back of the restaurant, is now a chef, restaurateur, and Food Network personality who goes by the name Jet Tila. Meanwhile, both Bangkok Market and the family restaurant, Royal Thai Cuisine, continue to serve the people of Los Angeles the very best Thai food.

Learning the Language

The English language is a struggle that all immigrants must confront in one way or another, and Thai immigrants are no different. Earlier, we mentioned Ittikorn Hunsagul, the architect who was washing dishes in a restaurant while learning English. His English as a Second Language (ESL) teacher told a reporter that "[Ittikorn's] determination is large, like a lot of my students... There is this great worker right there inside him. There is just this very thin but strong door called language."

Kao Kalia Yang wrote about her frustrations with English when she entered the first grade in North End Elementary School in St. Paul, Minnesota. She and her sister were placed in a special class for children who had recently arrived from Thailand's refugee camps. Her sister picked up English quite quickly, even winning a spelling bee in the third grade. But for Kao the situation was entirely different. She didn't mind writing in English but hated being forced to speak. "English was hard on my tongue.... My voice sounded different to me in English. I didn't like the way I stuttered and breathed through the words, so I tried never to speak unless it was necessary…. I got by with nodding and shaking my head and smiling."

Kao's experience is not uncommon. Teachers have observed that many young Thai immigrants are shy, and they are reluctant to make mistakes in class. One experienced teacher of English described this as "losing face. Thai students may feel that they could lose face by giving the wrong answer, so they say nothing." This is unfortunate because it creates a vicious circle—after all, the less you speak today, the less likely you are to try tomorrow.

There are also some specific challenges in going from spoken Thai to

Large demon statues guard the entrance to Los Angeles's Wat Thai temple.

spoken English. Thai doesn't use **intonation** in the same way English does. For example, it's not natural for a Thai speaker's voice to go up at the end of a question and down at the end of a statement. Certain English sounds just don't exist in Thai, and they can be difficult for Thai mouths to make, and even for Thai ears to understand. One teacher reported that, according to his Thai students, "It looks like rain" is the most difficult sentence in the English language! For her part, Kao's struggle with spoken English continued for several years, even as she excelled in written English.

 Got Rice?

Sometimes language and food go hand-in-hand. For instance, rice is so central to Thai culture that "How are you?" in Thai is "*Gin khao reu yung?*" Literally translated, that means, "Have you had rice yet?"

Rice is arguably the single most important component of any Thai meal. And Thai cuisine doesn't just use one type of rice; there are many types, and they all have their particular place in the Thai diet. The most famously "Thai" rice is probably sticky (or glutinous) rice. As its name suggests, it is gummier than the long-grain rice you know from Chinese food, and it can be picked up and eaten by hand. Thais also eat a lot of a certain type of long-grain white rice called *hom mali* (jasmine rice), which has a very distinctive aroma. There are also types of rice that are just for dessert; they come in intense shades of green, yellow, and blue.

Bridging the Culture Gap

Communication challenges for many Thai immigrants go beyond simply how words are pronounced. Thai people sometimes prefer to speak more indirectly; they don't just say what's on their mind, the way people do in the United States.

Observers have described Thais as being "**collectivist**" in nature, while Americans tend to be more "individualist." When we describe American culture as "individualist," we mean that Americans tend to focus on themselves and their immediate family; personal experiences, desires, and

These signs show some of the characters of the Thai language, evidence of the difficulty immigrants might have mastering English.

plans all tend to revolve around an individual and his or her immediate social circle. Cultures that are more collectivist—as Asian cultures generally tend to be—are more focused on the needs and demands of a whole group. It's not proper to put oneself forward as being particularly special.

Thai Food: Thailand vs. America

It isn't just people who have to adapt to a new country; their food adapts, too. Thai restaurants seem to be everywhere these days, but the food you enjoy at your local Thai place has changed a lot in its journey from Southeast Asia to your town. Here are just a few of the **accommodations** that Thai chefs have made to suit American taste buds.

Portion sizes	Smaller overall	Noticeably larger
Order of courses	There really isn't one; dinners are often served "family style," meaning everything is put out on the table all at once.	There is often a specific order of dishes: appetizer, soup or salad, main course, dessert.
Chopsticks	Thai people only eat noodles with chopsticks; forks, spoons, and knives are used for other dishes.	Some Americans avoid chopsticks at all costs, while others will use them to eat anything Asian, even when Asian people would not.
Meat	Occasional seafood or pork is included in meals, but it's not vital.	Usually a meat dish is the central part of meal.
Spice level	Pretty spicy, but balanced with other flavors.	Less spicy overall as compared to Thailand.
Sour flavor	Considered an important part of the balance of flavors.	Often avoided, as Americans tend not to like sour foods.

Kao Kalia Yang relates a perfect example of this conflict in her memoir, when she and her sister had to help their mother write a resume. The mother wanted the resume to state that "she would try her very best" at any new job, but the daughters argued that this wasn't nearly a strong-enough statement. In America, they explained, you need to say things like, "I *will* do great work"—it's not enough to say you'd simply *try*. That kind of declaration can be very difficult for people raised in collectivist societies to accept. It's not necessarily that they aren't confident, but it would be considered impolite to brag in that way.

Kids and Parents

In general, children acclimate themselves to new surroundings more quickly than adults do. They learn the language more quickly, and they are quicker to pick up local customs and habits.

The result is that immigrant kids end up having to help their parents a lot more than non-immigrant kids do—for instance, asking where certain things are in a store. As Kao Kalia Yang put it, "We [the kids] became the interpreters and translators for our family dealings with American people.... We just did it because it was easier and because we did not want to see them struggle over easy things."

This often happens to young immigrants whose parents work in the restaurant business, like chef Jet Tila. As kids, they learned the family business whether they wanted to or not. For example, Andy and Anna Asapahu moved to Los Angeles from Thailand with their children, and they founded their restaurant, Ayara Thai, in 2004. Their eldest daughter, Vanda, is now grown and helping run the business she loves, but she didn't always appreciate all the hands-on experience she was getting. "From looking at tax papers at 10 years old, to calling for phone services," she told a reporter in 2017, "at a young age you learn and you get involved. I used to ask, 'Why do Sally's parents never make her learn any of this?'"

It makes sense that immigrant kids would pick up language and customs more quickly than adults, and it also makes sense that the kids would turn around and help translate for their parents. However, that can also lead to family conflicts. While parents naturally expect to be in charge at home, that structure is threatened when they depend on their children to help read the mail or answer the phone. Meanwhile, some kids secretly feel embarrassed that their parents need help with seemingly easy tasks.

Like all immigrants, Thai people want to become part of America.

Family conflicts can also arise over just how **integrated** a family is going to be. On the one hand, parents often make great sacrifices to give their children better lives in the United States. On the other hand, those same parents sometimes feel threatened by how "foreign" their children become. In *Talk Thai*, Ira Sukrunruang recalls the struggles that went on in his family as he became increasingly Americanized. "This is a Thai home," Ira's parents would often remind him. "You are Thai."

Yes, they wanted him to work hard and succeed in the new country, but not at the expense of his cultural identity. Nevertheless, he writes, "America secretly began invading our home, seeping through cracks underneath doors, climbing through open windows, like an invasive vine that devoured houses in the South." It is no accident that the cover of *Talk Thai* features young Ira dressed in his Superman costume, arms raised in victory like the American comic book hero he loved.

Text-Dependent Questions:

1. Why do some Thai immigrants struggle with English?

2. What types of rice are important in Thai cuisine?

3. What are some of the ways Thai food has been altered for American taste buds?

Research Project:

Find out more about the philosophy of collectivism. How might you live your life differently if you lived in a more collectivist country? Do you think you would like it? What parts might be better or worse? Would you miss aspects of the individualism of the United States?

THE MAIN COURSE

A Thai meal usually comprises rice and three or four dishes, served "family style," meaning all the plates are brought to the table and everyone takes what they like.

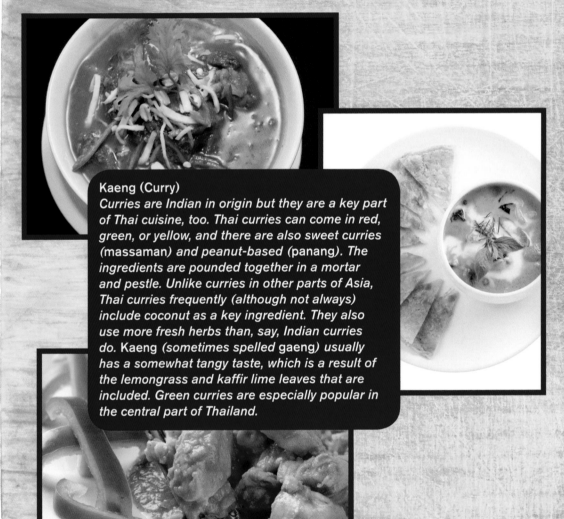

Kaeng (Curry)

Curries are Indian in origin but they are a key part of Thai cuisine, too. Thai curries can come in red, green, or yellow, and there are also sweet curries (massaman) and peanut-based (panang). The ingredients are pounded together in a mortar and pestle. Unlike curries in other parts of Asia, Thai curries frequently (although not always) include coconut as a key ingredient. They also use more fresh herbs than, say, Indian curries do. Kaeng (sometimes spelled gaeng) usually has a somewhat tangy taste, which is a result of the lemongrass and kaffir lime leaves that are included. Green curries are especially popular in the central part of Thailand.

Pad Krapow Moo Sap (Fried Basil and Pork)
In this spicy dish, minced, fatty pork is stir-fried along with lots of Thai basil, green beans, soy sauce, and a whole lot of chilis. Thai basil is different from the Italian basil you may be used to; it has purple stems, thinner leaves, and a more intense, almost licorice-like flavor. Pad krapow moo sap is often served with a fried egg on top.

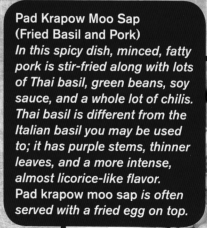

Pla Pao (Grilled Fish)
Common along Thailand's coasts, pla pao involves grilling fish whole. Usually the fish is stuffed with lemongrass and kaffir lime leaves and then the skin is crusted with salt before the fish is put on a not-too-hot grill and cooked slowly. It's served with a garlicky, spicy sauce called nam jim seafood.

4

Reaching Back

When that first group of Thai immigrants arrived in Los Angeles in the mid-1960s, their new city had no Buddhist *wat* (temple) where they could worship. As we've mentioned, this is why many ceremonies ended up being held at the Tilakamonkul family's market instead. But it wasn't long before Thai immigrants had built their own temple, Wat Thai in North Hollywood. Today Wat Thai is more popular than ever, and not just for Buddhists. On the weekends, the parking lot is transformed into an open-air food market and restaurant, with vendors selling what many people say is some of the best Thai food in the city.

Cultural institutions like Buddhist wats, as well as Thai markets and restaurants, continue to be places where Thai Americans can connect with their cultural identities while still remaining very much American.

Words to Understand

alms money or food given to the poor or, in this case, to monks
designate   to officially give someone or something a particular status

Buddhism is important to many Thai people, so having a temple like this one in Los Angeles helps them connect to their country far away.

Both Thai and American

Many first-generation Thai immigrants wanted to assimilate into their new country as much as possible. But as time passed, some of these newly minted Americans regretted having let go of their birth culture. Meanwhile, their Thai American children often wondered about their family background. The result has been an increased interest in reviving Thai language and cultural practices. Many wats have been at the center of this trend. For instance, a wat in Seattle offers classes in Thai language and traditional dance, as does the wat in Berkeley, California.

Some cultural organizations work in several directions at once, offering workshops to help recent immigrants get settled in America, while also helping Thai Americans learn more about Thailand's history, language,

 ## Boxing, Thai-Style

Although Thailand's most famous export has to be pad thai, Muay Thai boxing is a close second. Muay Thai is a kickboxing-like style of combat that developed in Thailand beginning in the 14th century. The basic concept of Muay Thai is that the entire body can be used as a weapon. Students learn a variety of punches and kicks with names like the Spinning Back Kick and the Superman Punch. Muay Thai classes are offered all over the United States, sometimes as part of a larger martial arts program, and sometimes as a standalone program.

and culture. For instance, the Thai Association of Southern California in Sun Valley offers classes in both Thai literacy *and* navigating the American real estate market. Similarly, the Thai American Association of Michigan provides services to both recently arrived immigrants and established Thai Americans who wish to reconnect with their ethnic background.

Two Cultures at Once

If you have ever visited a big city, you've probably heard of ethnic neighborhoods like Chinatown, Greek Town, or Little Italy. The only official Thai Town in the United States is a six-block area along Hollywood Boulevard in Los Angeles; the neighborhood was **designated** as Thai Town in 1999. The goals of Thai Town are twofold. First, the designation was a business decision, made in hopes of boosting tourism to the area; but the neighborhood also provides an opportunity to connect with Thai culture.

A food fair at Wat Thai temple

The restaurants there go beyond typical Thai food. For example, you can visit a restaurant that specializes in super-spicy food from the southern part of Thailand, or head around the corner to try Thai-style BBQ from the northern region, where pork is very popular. Thai Town also has supermarkets, sweet shops, and a Thai-centric bookstore. Orange-robed monks from Wat Thai can be seen on the streets, and they will offer blessings in exchange for **alms**.

But perhaps the most important contribution that Thai Town makes to the immigrant community is that it hosts a New Year's Festival every April. In Thailand, the new year is, in effect, celebrated twice: The country joins the rest of the world in observing January 1 as the beginning

 ## New Year Dishes

Many cultures observe traditions that are designed to increase luck for the coming new year, and Thai customs during Songkran are no different. The minced chicken salad dish called *larb gai* is considered a lucky New Year's dish; *larb* can be translated as "luck" in Thai. See page 35 for more about what's in the salad. Another food that may bring good luck is a type of dumpling called *toong tong*. Meat and spices are tied up in wonton wrappers and fried; literally translated, *toong tong* means "money bags."

of a new calendar year. But the lunar new year, known as Songkran, is celebrated in April and is by far the more important festival. (Songkran is observed across most of Southeast Asia as well as parts of China and India.) To celebrate Songkran, Thai Town in Los Angeles hosts a parade and other events that attract around 100,000 people every year.

While Los Angeles is the only American city with an official Thai Town, Sydney, Australia, has a Thai Town as well, located not far from its Chinatown. There are also many unofficial neighborhoods where Thai immigrants are more likely to gather, such as Elmhurst, a neighborhood in the Queens section of New York City, which has a lively collection of Thai restaurants and businesses.

This market in Sydney, Australia, is part of a vibrant Thai community.

Whether there's a Thai neighborhood nearby or not, the most significant aspect of this trend is psychological: It's the realization on the part of immigrants that there's no need to choose between being Thai or being American. As Seattle-based immigrant Sukapit "Duke" Bhuphaibool told a reporter in 2016, it was a revelation to him that he could be both fully American and also feel connected to the culture of his birth. After living in the United States for 30 years, he began attending wat for the first time in decades. "I realized that being Asian and being American aren't

Thai restaurants offer an inviting look at another culture.

exclusive," Bhuphaibool said. "When I came to America, I was told differently: To be Asian means that you're not American; to be American means you're not Asian...[but] I realized that I could be American and I could be Thai."

Text-Dependent Questions:

1. What are wats and what roles do some of them play for Thai immigrants?

2. Where can you find some official and unofficial Thai towns?

3. What is Songkran?

Research Project:

Find out more about the rich histories of ethnic neighborhoods like Chinatowns or Little Italys. What purpose did these neighborhoods serve originally, and what purpose do they serve now? If you live close enough to a city, try and visit one or more of its ethnic neighborhoods. What do you notice about them?

DESSERT

Many aspects of Thai cuisine might seem foreign to Americans but dessert should not be one of them! Thai people have quite the sweet tooth and they enjoy a wide variety of sweet treats.

Khao Niao Mamuang (Mango Sticky Rice)
In the United States, we don't tend to associate rice with dessert, but in Thai cuisine, sticky rice is often part of sweet treats. It can be paired with all kinds of tasty ingredients, but mango is probably the most popular.

Gluay Kag (Fried Bananas)
In Thailand, fried bananas are sold by street vendors as a snack. Here in the United States, on the other hand, you'll usually find them on the dessert menus of Thai restaurants. Frequently they are served with ice cream on the side. Some people use plantains rather than bananas, because the flavor and texture of plantains are a closer match to the type of bananas found in Thailand.

I Tim Pad (Rolled Ice Cream)

Also called "ice pan" ice cream, i tim pad is a fairly new but wildly popular dessert both in Thailand and all over the world. It is also called stir-fried, but it's not actually "fried." To make it, milk and other ingredients are spread thin across a super-cold pan and mixed together using metal spatulas. Then the ice cream is rolled and served in a bowl along with toppings. Watching the process of making i tim pad is almost as much fun as eating it, and there are lots of internet videos that show rolled ice cream being made.

DESSERT

Luk Chup (Fruit-Shaped Mung Beans)
In an old European dessert called marzipan, almonds are ground up into a paste, combined with sugar, and then transformed into any kind of shape or object you can imagine. Portuguese traders brought marzipan to Thailand in the 17th century, and the Thais responded by inventing their own version, luk chup. *Almonds aren't common in Thailand, so Thai chefs used green mung beans instead. The beans are made into a paste along with sweet ingredients such as coconut milk, and then they are molded into shapes. Most often,* luk chup *is made to look like tiny fruits and vegetables, but it can be made into anything, such as cute little pigs or ducks. Originally* luk chup *was a dessert only for royalty, but today it can be found in grocery stores across Thailand, as well as in some Asian markets and sweet shops in the West.*

RECIPE

Kai Jeow (Thai Omelet)

Thai-style omelets are made very quickly on very high heat. They should be crispy on the outside and creamy on the inside, and it doesn't matter what shape they are.

Ingredients:
   2 eggs
   1/2 teaspoon lime juice
   1 teaspoon Thai fish sauce
   1 tablespoon water
   1 tablespoon cornstarch
   vegetable oil

Steps:

• *Combine the eggs, lime juice, fish sauce, water, and cornstarch. Beat with a fork and make sure there are no lumps of cornstarch left.*

• *Heat oil on high in a wok or, if you don't have one, a flat-bottomed saucepan. You need a fair amount of oil—between 1/2 and 3/4 cup, depending on the size of the pan. It needs to be enough oil to cover the bottom of the pan and be about a quarter of an inch deep. Heat until the oil is extremely hot and starting to smoke.*

• *Hold the egg mixture high over the pan and pour it in all at once. After 30 seconds, flip the omelet and cook for another 30 seconds.*

• *Remove from heat and enjoy with jasmine rice and sriracha sauce.*

Find Out More

Books

Leap High School: Green Card Youth Voices: Immigration Stories from a St. Paul High School. Minneapolis, MN: Wise Ink Creative Publishing, 2017.

Sukrungruang, Ira. *Talk Thai: The Adventures of a Buddhist Boy.* Columbia, MO: University of Missouri, 2010.

Thompson, David. *Thai Food.* Berkeley, CA: Ten Speed Press, 2002.

Yang, Kao Kalia. *The Latehomecomer: A Hmong Family Memoir.* Minneapolis, MN: Coffee House Press, 2008.

Websites

https://migrationology.com/?s=thailand
 A great food blog by Mark Wiens with thoughtful and fun articles about many different aspects of Thai food.

http://www.visitasianla.org/index.php/thai-town
Lots of information about Thai Town, including a calendar of upcoming events

https://www.thespruce.com/exploring-thai-food-4128488
Learn about Thai food and culture, including recipes and how to choose unfamiliar ingredients.

Series Glossary of Key Terms

acclimate to get used to something

assimilate become part of a different society, country, or group

bigotry treating the members of a racial or ethnic group with hatred and intolerance

culinary having to do with the preparing of food

diaspora a group of people who live outside the area in which they had lived for a long time or in which their ancestors lived

emigrate leave one's home country to live in another country

exodus a mass departure of people from one place to another

first-generation American someone born in the United States whose parents were foreign-born

immigrants those who enter another country intending to stay permanently

naturalize to gain citizenship, with its rights and privileges

oppression a system of forcing people to follow rules or a system that restricts freedoms

presentation in this series, the style in which food is plated and served

Index

assimilation, 8, 38, 45, 52
Australia, 18, 26, 32-33, 55
Bangkok Market, 39-40
boxing, 52
Buddhists, 50
Chang and Eng, 18
children, 45-47, 52
chili peppers, 13-14
classes, 53
Colombo Plan, 17-18
cuisine, 12, 14, 22-23, 34-35, 42, 48-49, 58-61
cultural differences, 43-47
desserts, 58-61
education, 26-29, 38, 40-42
Elmhurst, 55

ethnic backgrounds, 52-53
ethnic cleansing, 29-30
exclusion acts, 20
family conflicts, 46-47
Farang, 15
flavors, 14
fried rice, 19, 23
history, 6-8, 15-17, 19
Hmong people, 30
holidays, 54-55
immigration to America, 18-21, 24, 26, 28-29
ingredients, 13-14, 38-39
Jet Tila, 40, 45
jobs, 27-29
Karen people, 30, 33
Kingdom of Aytthaya, 15

language, 38, 40-43, 45-46, 52-53
Los Angeles, 6, 39-40, 50, 55
main courses, 48-49
markets, 39-40, 50
marriage, 18-19, 38
meal presentations, 14-15
Muay Thai, 52
Myanmar, 32
New Year's Dishes, 54
Pad Thai, 22
population, 12, 21
recipes, 39
refugee camps, 30, 32-33
restaurants, 27, 29, 40, 50, 54-55
rice, 42
Royal Thai Cuisine, 40

Siam, Narai (King), 16
Siamese twins, 18
sociologists, 29
Songkran, 55
soups and salads, 34-35
spring rolls, 22
Sriracha, 31
stir-fry, 12-13
street food, 22-23
students, 17-18
temples see Wats
terrorists, 32-33
Thai American food, 14
Thai communities, 6, 21
Thai Town, 53-55
Tom Kha Gai, 35
Vietnam War, 18-20
water bugs, 23
Wats, 50, 52, 54, 56

Photo Credits

Dreamstime.com: Dimaberkut 7; Erik Lattwein 8; Sompote Saalee 12; Somyot Pattana 13; Kritiya 15; Somboon Temchuen 16; Supanee Hickman 20; Yanukit Sujjariyarux 22T; Dianearbis 22B; Mitrs3 23T; Boysitti 23C; Baghitsha 23B; Dontree 25; Gow927 26, 28; Ame9001 27; Bhofack2 31; Jinying Du 32; Piman Khrutmuang 34T; Taweepat Larpparisut 34B; Mihai Ursea 35T; Benjamin Dupont 35C; Agneskantaruk 35B; MBI 37; JGHunter 41; Elzbieta Kiatpanapukul 43; Nopparat Jaikla 48T; Kaiskynet 48C; Quentin Bargate 48B; Panuwat T. 49T; Chris De Bug 49; Bennn 52; Thuatha22 54; Saard Saenmuang 56; Matee Nuserm 58T; VM2002 58B; Marveric Rabina 59; Oilslo 60T; Kenisirotie 60B. Newscom: Chris Polydoroff/KRT 11; Gary Porter/KRT 30. Shutterstock: Braydon Howle 17; Ronnachai Palas 46; Danuponphotographer 51; ArliftAtoZ2205 55.

Author Bio

H.W. Poole is a writer and editor of books for young people, including the sets *Childhood Fears and Anxieties*, *Families Today*, and *Mental Illnesses and Disorders* (Mason Crest). She created the *Horrors of History* series (Charlesbridge) and the *Ecosystems* series (Facts On File). She was coauthor and editor of *The History of the Internet* (ABC-CLIO), which won the 2000 American Library Association RUSA award.